LET'S SIGN Early Years
2nd Edition
BSL Building Blocks
Child and Carer Guide

FROM CO-SIGN COMMUNICATIONS
(INC. DEAFSIGN & DEAFBOOKS)

SIGN LANGUAGE LINK: A Pocket Dictionary of Signs

SIGNS OF HEALTH: A Pocket Medical Sign Language Guide

THE LET'S SIGN SERIES

LET'S SIGN BSL TUTOR PACK: Tutor book and CD-Rom

LET'S SIGN BSL Greetings Signs and Fingerspelling A2 Wallchart

LET'S SIGN BSL Poster/Mats A4 Set of 4
Greetings-Family-Feelings-Questions

LET'S SIGN A4 Bildtafeln zur (4)
Deutschen Gebärdensprache
Tätigkeiten - Familie - Fragen - Gefühle

LET'S SIGN FOR WORK: BSL Guide for Service Providers - 2nd Edition

LET'S SIGN BSL EARLY YEARS & BABY SIGNS: Poster/Mats A3 Set of 2

LET'S SIGN BSL FLASHCARDS: Early Years & Baby Signs

LET'S SIGN BSL THANK YOU CARDS

LET'S SIGN BSL CHILDREN'S FINGERSPELLING CHART

LET'S SIGN POCKET DICTIONARY: BSL Concise Beginner's Guide

LET'S SIGN FAMILY TOPICS: BSL for Children and their Carers

LET'S SIGN & DOWN SYNDROME: Signs for Children with Special Needs

A CHILD'S BOOK OF SIGNED PRAYERS

LET'S SIGN SCIENCE: BSL Vocabulary for KS 1, 2, & 3 (Dictionary)

LET'S SIGN BSL Graphics Packs *for Science, Early Years and General*

LET'S SIGN SONGS FOR CHILDREN: Popular Songs to Sign-a-long to

LET'S SIGN BSL FLASHCARDS: House & Home

LET'S SIGN BSL REWARD STICKERS

LET'S SIGN BSL EARLY YEARS CURRICULUM TUTOR BOOK & CD

LET'S SIGN BSL EARLY YEARS CURRICULUM STUDENT BOOK

**(Many of the above publications are also available in electronic and
mobile applications and Kindle format)**

LET'S SIGN Early Years
2nd Edition
BSL Building Blocks
Child and Carer Guide

CATH SMITH and SANDRA TEASDALE
Illustrated by Cath Smith

CO-SIGN COMMUNICATIONS

First published (1st edition) 2003 Reprinted 2004 (twice) 2005 (twice) 2007, 2009, 2011 (ISBN: 0954238419)

2nd Edition Revised and Colour Version 2012

ISBN-13: 9781905913220

ISBN-10: 1905913222

Published by Co-Sign Communications
(inc.Deafsign & DeafBooks)
16 Highfield Crescent, Hartburn,
Stockton-on-Tees TS18 5HH

Tel: 01642 580505
email: cath@deafsign.com
www.DeafBooks.co.uk

Distributed by Gardners Books, Eastbourne

Printed in Great Britain by Alphagraphics
Stockton-on-Tees

ACKNOWLEDGEMENTS

Grateful thanks and appreciation go to;

Our families for being constant reminders of the importance of family.

Elizabeth Archibald, Teacher of the Deaf, for the many years of support and encouragement.

Adèle Marshall of Plymouth, Devon, for Signing With Babies information.

Robert Riley, graphic designer for his technical help with preparation of the 1st edition.

Stephen Smith, printer for his innovations, hard work and commitment.

Cover photographs for 2nd Edition by kind permission of Elsie Smith, Rachel Middleton and William Smith.

*Welcome to the 2nd edition of **Let's Sign Early Years**. In the nine years since first publication in 2003 this book has proved a ground-breaking and popular publication for families and carers of children who are deaf or who have additional language and communication needs and those who wish their child to learn the basics of one of Britain's community languages to enhance their own development.*

This book has provided invaluable support for all those wishing to learn and teach British Sign Language (BSL) with children, when little else was available in this country. On completing the full revision and conversion to colour we note that the contents have stood the test of time well - there is little to change within the information, choice of vocabulary and the signs chosen.

CONTENTS

INTRODUCTION

Introducing Sandra Teasdale

I was born profoundly deaf and I work with families of pre-school deaf children. My first language is British Sign Language (BSL), which I am using now to introduce myself - it will be changed into English for the book.

BSL is my first language, even though my parents and family didn't sign and I had very little access to it when I was small. It is the language that feels natural and comfortable to me, and the only way I can express myself properly.

Like my *Deaf friends and colleagues, English is not easy for me. I go about my daily life in the outside world and that is not a problem. I am totally used to mixing with hearing people, and manage perfectly well with my life - setting up and running our own home with my husband, dealing with our daughters' education and welfare, driving, shopping and all the normal everyday things of life. But if I have to communicate for any length, or write something out in full English, I use interpreting support, otherwise it's a great strain and makes me very unsure of myself.

I know how important English is, as it's the language of the hearing world around us, and that we were born into, but it is not my first language, and it never will be, and the same is true for some of the deaf children of today.

* The convention of the upper case 'D' in *Deaf* refers to people who identify themselves as culturally Deaf sign language users.

I grew up and went to school at a time when BSL was not heard of. Not because it wasn't there, but because it hadn't been recognised and accepted as a language. There are times when I think this is still the same.

Like all deaf schools in this country and others, sign language was strictly forbidden at my school. That didn't stop us from signing though - because signing was the only way we could communicate, and we all signed at school, between ourselves and when the teacher's head was turned - otherwise we just didn't know what was going on.

I suppose it must have given us a tremendous bond too, and most of us have remained life long friends, including the boy I went out with in my teens, who is now my husband.

Not all of the children at the school were totally deaf, there was a real mixture, just as there is today. Some had a lot of hearing and speech, and used their hearing aids to communicate in this way - they were lost without them. Others had some useful hearing, that they could use in some situations, but needed lip-reading (and signs) to help too - some could speak quite clearly and others couldn't.

Then there were others like myself who could only pick up here and there through lip-reading - nothing through hearing aids. We relied on information being passed on by the others with better hearing and could sign to us.

The important point is that we all signed - and those who spoke still spoke - signing never stopped them.

During my time at school, we only ever had one teacher who signed to us. This was towards the end of our time at school, but it was wonderful. This teacher, like the others, had been trained at university to believe that using sign language would stop us from speaking and learning English. It would make us 'lazy' and rely on signs (which wasn't a 'proper' language). Because we live in a hearing world, and must go on and work and spend our lives with people who only communicate through spoken language, we simply had to learn it too, even though we were deaf. And of course, some of the others could - and did do that, so if we tried hard enough, then we all should be able to.

Then this teacher became involved with the Deaf community, and started to listen to those who had a different point of view entirely. She started to listen to those who worked in that community, and to Deaf people themselves, and that changed everything for her.

After that, the door would be firmly closed, to stop prying eyes, and so that there were no interruptions. That was always how she worked anyway, as she took her lessons very seriously, and did not welcome people popping in and out and distracting things.

Everything came alive for us in that time - we could follow what she was teaching us, it became full of meaning, it was interesting and exciting.

I was also lucky, because there were a number of Deaf families where I grew up. Some families had a Deaf mum and dad, as well as themselves, and my own hearing parents used to encourage me to mix with them. It was great to go round to their houses where they all signed. I remember my friend's father, who was also profoundly deaf, explaining to me what was going on in the news that was on TV. Pointing to the screen, and then turning to sign and explain what was happening - it opened up a whole new world for me, and I was very lucky as many deaf children never experience this. You can see it in their parents' eyes as they get near a Deaf person, and clutch their child's hand to draw them away. Imagine what that feels like.

I do understand why that happens - I have worked with families for long enough to understand that parents can feel very threatened and uncertain when with Deaf people. Part of it is the communication barrier, but mostly they are fearful that they will in some way lose their child to the Deaf world. They feel that we are something different, alien, and they can't relate that to their own child.

This is so wrong - we have so much to offer.

We Deaf people see deaf children, and we know exactly what it's like. We feel drawn to other Deaf - adults and children, because we know what it's like and have so much in common, and we just want to share that.

It is slowly changing, as more families are finding, or being given opportunities, to meet with Deaf adults, and it also makes a difference having chance to meet a Deaf person who is working in education too. When I first became involved, before I was appointed onto the staff of the Hearing Impaired Service, I was a volunteer in a local pre-school parents' group at the Deaf Centre, set up by a hearing teacher.

The teacher chose the Deaf Club as a link between our two worlds, and thought that it was very important for the mothers (because there were no fathers attending at that time) to meet Deaf people. She encouraged me all the way to get involved, and I'm so glad that that happened. She didn't force me on the parents, or them on me, she just set the scene, and let things happen naturally.

At first the mothers were very unsure, and cautious around me. It was, after all, a very new experience for them, and for me too for that matter. I was there to look after the children, and the teacher brought lots of lovely, bright interesting toys and games. I took my own 2 year old hearing daughter with me too. Slowly, the mums starting watching me with the children. How I got their eye contact - tapping their arm or shoulder - or waving a hand slightly in their line of vision, and how I held and kept their interest in our play, and especially, I think, how I used my face to show my feelings and relate to the children.

I didn't know I was particularly doing any of these things, I was just doing what came naturally to me as a Deaf person.

Gradually, they became less shy, and encouraged me to come over and talk to them, asking how to sign little phrases - 'don't cry' 'mummy loves you' and so, on, or how to play counting games - just simple things. My own daughter was a help too, because they could see that she was perfectly at home with all this. Sign language was her first language, and she quickly developed English alongside it, through her contacts with both sets of hearing grandparents, and nursery and so on, to become fully bi-lingual.

I think that this involvement, of Deaf and hearing people together, is the best way forward for families and children, and I hope that these details of my own experiences make sense to others and is of help to them too.

I want my message to be simple. Please sign with your child - there is nothing to lose, and everything to gain - and please let it be BSL.

Introducing the SIGNWELLS

Liz — Hello and welcome — Anu

Will — Ben — Rose — Omar

To LET'S SIGN: EARLY YEARS

Amy — Jed — Tom

Please read and enjoy

We hope that our characters add fun and interest to your learning, and have added their names to help with the fingerspelling practice as suggested on page 34. In Deaf culture, people are usually allocated name signs based on personal characteristics, traits or interests. Anu might be given the name sign 'hair in bunches', for example, or Rose 'flower'.

BRITISH SIGN LANGUAGE
It Makes Sense

Interest in sign language comes from many sources. This book focuses on the use of signs with deaf children but even greater numbers of adults and children with special educational needs (SEN) now learn through BSL signs too and use the Let's Sign BSL Series of resources to support this.

Children with learning disability and additional speech, language and communication needs associated with, for example, Down's syndrome, autism and cerebral palsy, are taught using speech and BSL signs simultaneously. This is known as Sign Supported English (SSE), a form of BSL used within the community and also as part of BSL use in deaf education when situations and individual needs require it.

Signing with babies is also gaining popularity. Following studies in America, sign language is now thought to benefit all children's development, helping to provide communication with pre-verbal infants, and bringing visual and kinaesthetic elements, which add extra dimensions to language and communication that some children are extremely responsive to, and all children can potentially benefit from. (See Signing With Babies page 119.)

There are also others - parents of hearing children, who want their children to learn BSL as a second language, just as they might learn French or German in school - because they believe it will benefit their own child's development and because they think it is a more useful language to have. There is also exciting development work with BSL key word support for children for whom English is not a first language.

This groundswell of interest in, and respect for BSL from the majority culture is greatly welcome, but it is also ironic that in its long history of oppression, BSL has been banned from deaf educational use with the very children who need it most.

This has been the experience of generations of Deaf people who form the linguistic minority culture of the Deaf community, and to whom BSL belongs.

The inclusion of BSL in deaf education is a recent development and in spite of the misconception that all deaf children use sign language, BSL is used by less than 10% of deaf children, due partly to lingering beliefs that signing will hinder spoken language development, in spite of evidence to the contrary.

In March 2003 a Government announcement recognised BSL as a language in its own right. This brought increased expectations for the use of BSL in deaf children's education. In 2003 when this book was first published, 92% of deaf children were being educated in mainstream schools, only some of which had special units and 79% of deaf children were being educated by oral/aural methods that exclude sign language.

The most recent details available at time of writing this 2nd edition are contained in the survey on educational provision for deaf children in England by the Consortium for Research into Deaf Education (CRIDE) report 2011.

Summary of key findings

• There are at least 34,927 deaf children in England.
• Around 19% have some form of additional special educational need (SEN).
• Around 6% of deaf children have at least one cochlear implant.
• 15% of deaf children communicate in part using a spoken language other than English. **9% use sign language to some extent to communicate.**
• 81% of school aged children are in mainstream settings (of which 8% are in mainstream schools with resource provision). 6% attend special schools for deaf children or independent schools. 12% attend other special schools.

15

STARTING WITH BSL

Sign languages are used all over the world, but they are not all the same language. They share similar structures but have their own vocabularies and variations.

BSL is structured and complex, just like any language. Like any language it is also learnable.

The earlier you start to sign with your child, the better. The pre-school years are the optimum time for language development.

A first language isn't 'taught', but is acquired through meaningful exchanges and interactions in an appropriate medium.

Early access to spoken and signed language with equal status for both, gives deaf children the chance to become bi-cultural and bi-lingual, for healthy adjustment as part of the Deaf and hearing worlds.

Seek advice as widely as you can and learn from Deaf people. Try to find family friendly classes.

You are an individual and so is your child. You know your child best, so trust your instincts.

Children have innate ability in language, and are able to make their own constructions from even very basic input from an early age.

Eye-contact is paramount in communication with deaf children, and this may be very fleeting, so you need to pack in as much as possible.

Signs are more densely packed than words. Nodding the head in affirmation, shaking in negation, raising the eyebrows in question form, can all take place simultaneously with sign productions.

Keep responses simple and compact.

Make comments then point if you want to draw your child's attention to something. Pointing first will lose eye contact as your child looks at what you point to.

Practice ways to gain and prolong eye-contact.

Eye-contact and face-reading are also important for the development of rapport and empathy.

Don't grasp the chin and turn a child's head to face you. Gain attention by gently tapping the arm, shoulder, or leg. Try not to approach from behind without some visual warning like flashing the lights on and off, stamping on the floor to make vibrations, banging on a table, or make small waving movements in the child's line of vision.

Accept your child's attempts at signs, and keep your own consistent.

Try to create a lively and colourful signing environment. Encourage friends and family to sign when around your child. Include brothers, sisters, aunties uncles and grandparents.

Think visually, and use your imagination.

USING LET'S SIGN

This introductory book offers signs and information that we hope will be of interest and use to as wide a readership as possible.

We have tried to include the important concept signs suitable for young children in the home, at nursery, and many other situations. Inevitably it will not have all the signs you might be needing, but the section on the creative use of classifying handshapes, and fingerspelling should provide further help.

We hope you can use the illustrations and characters to point things out, ask questions and so on, to encourage communication and language development eg.....

Ben's sorry..............why? Was Ben naughty?

Amy's crying perhaps she fell over?

Will's tired......... was he late to bed? Maybe.

Anu's sick .... Anu needs the doctor.

Who's in trouble? ....Who broke the toy?

Encourage your child to question and use their imagination.

Understanding and communication are what matters. Don't be afraid to experiment and improvise with sign production - make it large and clear - learn to play more visually, as Deaf people do with children, and make it fun.

GUIDE TO HEADINGS AND CAPTIONS

Languages do not always have direct word for word equivalents between each other, and the headings given for each sign are a guide to the sign's main meaning. The sign might have additional meanings, or there may be other signs for the same word.

In addition, certain BSL signs are subject to considerable variations either by region, the context they are used in, or simply individual choice. We have included illustrated examples or descriptions of such variations in the captions when appropriate and where space allows, which can be checked with Deaf BSL users for local use in your own area.

The captions also give extra information on the handshape, location and movement of signs.

Details of non-manual features (**facial/bodily expressions**) **variation,** and changes in **context** are given in **bold text** and additional meanings are given in *bold italics*.

Signs and fingerspelling are described and illustrated as if the signer is right-handed, with the right hand always referred to as R. and the left hand as L.

Left-handed signers will use the reverse of this, with the left hand as dominant.

From the thumb, the fingers are referred to as index, middle, ring and little finger.

DIRECTION, ORIENTATION
AND MOVEMENT

Terms used to describe the direction in which the hands face, point or move are given here. Description of hand orientation is based on the direction in which the palm faces regardless of whether the hand is open or closed.

As illustrated here, the R. hand is palm left and the L. hand is palm right, or they can also be described as palm facing, or palm in.

The hand may be described as '*pointing*' up, forward etc. even if the fingers are bent in a different direction or closed.

As illustrated, both hands are pointing forward, palms facing.

Diagonal movements are described '*forward/left*' or '*back/right*' and so on.

Some signs start with a full description of handshape and position before movement is made. This is then called a **formation**, which means they keep their position together as they move.

BASIC HANDSHAPES

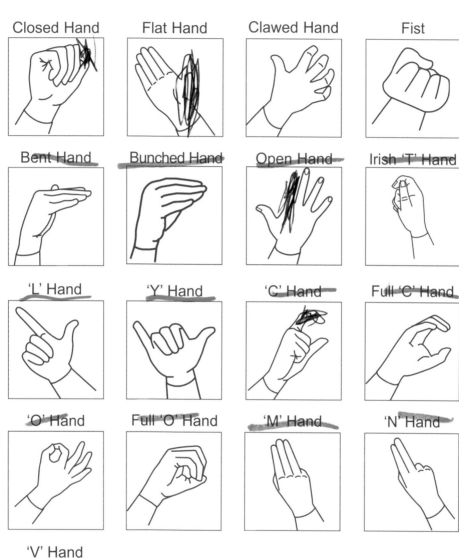

Closed Hand   Flat Hand   Clawed Hand   Fist

Bent Hand   Bunched Hand   Open Hand   Irish 'T' Hand

'L' Hand   'Y' Hand   'C' Hand   Full 'C' Hand

'O' Hand   Full 'O' Hand   'M' Hand   'N' Hand

'V' Hand

These are frequently used handshapes in BSL and the terms used in this book to describe them. If the handshapes are described for example as **index, middle finger and thumb extended**, then it is understood that the other fingers are closed.

21

BSL HANDSHAPES - CLASSIFIERS
Handling and Grasping

Sign vocabulary as shown in this book is from the established or fixed lexicon of BSL, similar to the words of spoken language. However, this is only part of the story. BSL is much less word based than English, and has great flexibility and creativity to enable new signs to be generated. Understanding some of this process is of great value to those new to BSL who may find themselves in immediate need of signs, helping them to create meaningful combinations on the spot, as they are needed.

The previous page shows basic handshapes and the terms used in this book to describe them. There are other important handshapes used in BSL that are known as **CLASSIFIERS**.

Some spoken languages make use of classifiers too, to signify groups with specific characteristics, eg objects with flat sides. BSL has a range of handshapes that work in a similar way, and can be used to refer to actions and objects based on their physical size, shape or outline, or how they are grasped, handled and moved. There are over 40 handshapes identified as classifiers, and 3 are illustrated here with examples of their use.

The Closed Hand or Fist

Occurs in signs based on holding/using cylindrical objects, handles or thick materials.

ice-cream

brush

drink (mug)

fridge

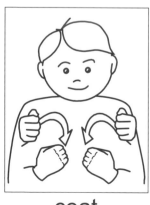

coat

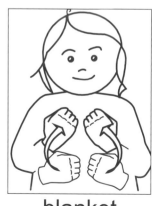

blanket

The Irish T Hand

(Named after the letter 'T' handshape from the Irish one-handed fingerspelling alphabet.)

Occurs in signs based on holding/using narrow flat or cylindrical objects that need finer control, or medium materials.

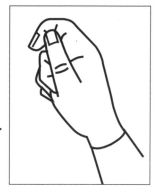

lolly

comb

toothbrush

key

umbrella

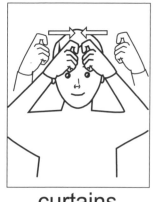

curtains

The O Hand

Occurs in signs based on holding/using very small or delicate objects, and fine or thin materials.

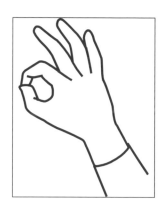

flower

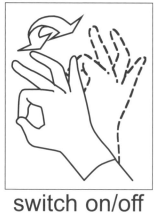

switch on/off

crisps

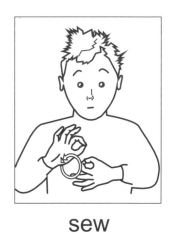

sew

teabag

sheet

SIGNS IN CONTEXT
Directional Verbs

Like words in spoken language, signs vary a great deal in context when in fluent use. There are a number of verbs that change direction to correspond with the subject and object in the situation they are being used. These are 2 simple examples of verbs **HELP** and **GIVE**. The signs on the left show *I help, I give* moving forwards from the signer, and on the right *help me, give me,* moving back towards the signer.

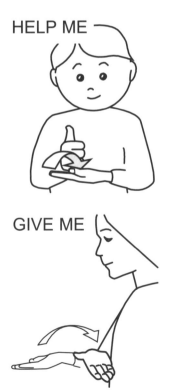

SIGNS IN CONTEXT
Inflections

Other signs can be inflected to make visual sense in context. These examples show the 'V' hand used to represent the direction and movement of eye-gaze in context. It moves forward from near the eye in **LOOK;** in small sideways wavy movements for **LOOK AROUND;** it twists sharply back to signer for **LOOK AT ME,** and sweeps up and down in **LOOK UP AND DOWN**, and infinite other possibilities in context.

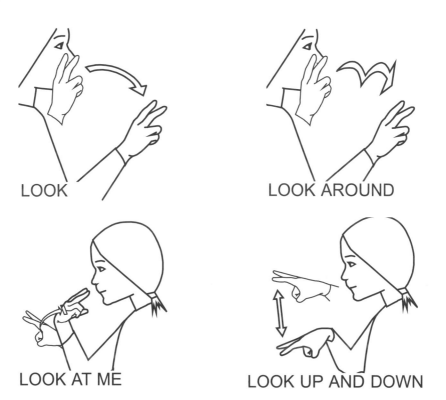

LOOK

LOOK AROUND

LOOK AT ME

LOOK UP AND DOWN

IT'S IN YOUR FACE
The Importance of Non-Manual Features

Learning BSL involves learning a whole new language, and in spite of popular myth and wishful thinking, this language is not universal. The vocabulary of signs is unique to BSL, and obviously an important part of the process, but much of the expressiveness we already possess is a crucial factor too.

One of the most important features of BSL is termed **NON-MANUAL FEATURES** (signed here in the first example). This refers to the expressive use of face and body that adds information to the manual signs made by the hands.

The good news for learners is that recent research shows that reading faces *is* a universal phenomenon, and that the conscious and unconscious messages we give out in this way would be understood the world over.

Learners typically home in on the hands and movements of the signs, often temporarily forgetting their natural ability to convey meaning non verbally, and yet it is the face that is the starting point and the focus for communicating in BSL. Attention is focused on the eyes, lip-patterns and expressions whilst the signing is taken in by peripheral vision.

In addition to relevant information such as concern, fear, anger and so on, non-manual features in BSL can give very specific grammatical information too. For example, puffed cheeks are used to emphasise intensity - an important part of the process of compacting extra detail into signs.

If part of the face is obscured - by dark glasses, beard, moustache, or surgical mask, for example, then reading meaning becomes much more difficult.

28

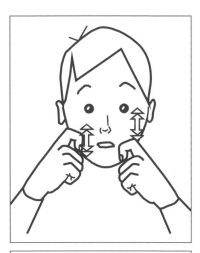

IT'S NOT WHAT YOU SIGN
IT'S THE WAY THAT YOU SIGN IT!

Look at these pictures and the ones on the page opposite. See how your face can change what you mean even though the sign is the same?

enough

enough?

more

more?

WHAT OUR FACE SAYS

You can question, or agree, or disagree. See how the face changes the meaning in these signs to make 'who?' become 'someone'. Can you see the difference?

enough!

who?

more!

someone

NUMBERS

There is wide variety in the way numbers are signed in BSL, but the following 1 - 10 number signs are based on the two most commonly used and understood systems used in Britain.

In adult signing, usually only one hand is used, so that 6 - 10 shown opposite would normally involve the R. hand only with the little finger, or bent thumb extended for 6 for example.

For introducing the concept of numbers to young children it is recommended that two hands are used as illustrated, progressing to one hand as the child develops.

0

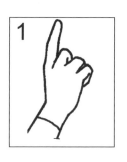
1

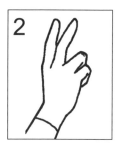
2

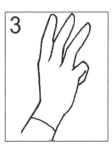
3

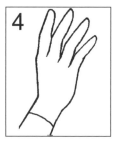
4

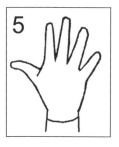
5

In these examples, the R. hand indicates 5, as the L. hand begins at the little finger, then little and ring finger, and so on to 9 - **OR** extended thumb (bent in 6) then thumb and index and so on to 9, with both hands used for 10.

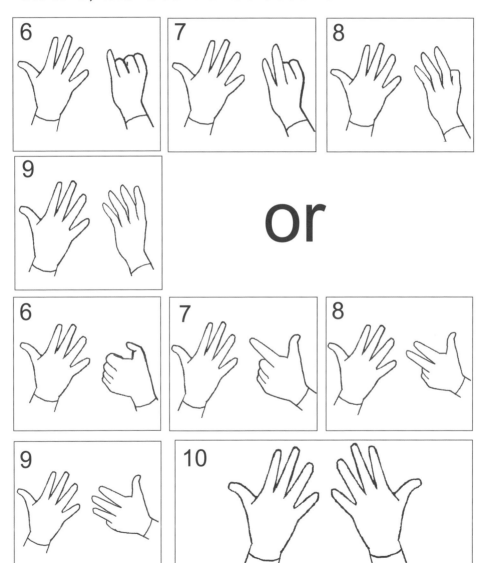

or

ABOUT FINGERSPELLING

Fingerspelling represents each letter of the alphabet on the hands and can be used to spell out whole words, abbreviated forms or initials.

It is rarely used to spell out whole phrases or sentences, but is commonly used for names and places. It can be easily learned but needs a lot of practice to read back and to develop the rhythms and patterns that fluent use produces and that make it an important and integrated part of BSL.

Fingerspelling was used in some Deaf schools even when sign language was not allowed, with seemingly good educational results although there are no modern studies. Its potential in education in many quarters has remained unexplored and perhaps underestimated, along with an assumption that you can't use fingerspelling with a child who doesn't yet know the alphabet.

Children in Deaf families are able to acquire fingerspelling ability from a very early age, recognising the sign-like shapes, patterns and rhythms long before they are familiar with the letters of the written alphabet, and it is this patterning rather than individual letters of an alphabet that are the key. The link to the written alphabet comes later - with fingerspelling an obvious link to literacy. As with all children's language development - you need plenty of input before you can expect any output, so it needs practice and perseverance.

Use of initial letters for names is useful, but quickly becomes limited, so the characters in the drawings have been given names to provide a useful starting point for practice with 3 and 4 letter names.

Start with just one or two, and practice them until you feel confident. For example, take the names **Amy** or **Ben**. Hold your hands loosely facing yourself, don't twist them to face forwards. Spell the names smoothly as you mouth or say the full names **AMY**, **BEN** (don't mouth individual letters 'A' 'M' 'Y' 'B"E"N'). Keep repeating, with a slight pause on the last letter, and gradually pick up speed - you will feel a rhythm and pattern starting to emerge.

Now try **Amy** and **Anu**, and see and feel the different pattern - much more advantage than initial letters alone. **Will** makes a lovely distinctive pattern, with the 'W' and the double bounce of the final 'LL' that matches its ease of lip-reading too.

Later, as you and your child progress, try some other simple words too - *car, bus* for example or *cat* and *dog*, sign them and spell them when you have the opportunity in context.

Bear in mind that attention and eye contact may be very fleeting, and use initials and contractions if it's more appropriate. Go with whatever you feel most comfortable with and which brings the best response.

BRITISH FINGERSPELLING ALPHABET
LEFT-HANDED VERSION

Aa	Bb

Cc	Dd	Ee	Ff

Gg	Hh	Ii	Jj

Kk	Ll	Mm	Nn

Oo	Pp	Qq	Rr

Ss	Tt	Uu	Vv

Ww	Xx	Yy	Zz

BRITISH FINGERSPELLING ALPHABET
RIGHT-HANDED VERSION

Aa	Bb

Cc	Dd	Ee	Ff

Gg	Hh	Ii	Jj

Kk	Ll	Mm	Nn

Oo	Pp	Qq	Rr

Ss	Tt	Uu	Vv

Ww	Xx	Yy	Zz

EXAMPLES OF SIGNS IN EVERYDAY USE

Wake up.........hello!   Good   boy/girl

Good   sleep?   Ready for breakfast?

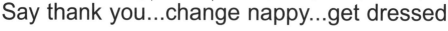

Say thank you...change nappy...get dressed

Go for a walk...... to the park....... see Nana.

EXAMPLES OF SIGNS IN EVERYDAY USE

Careful............ hot...........Don't touch!

You fell over?......... hurt ......where?....

You're cut .... Get a plaster.......

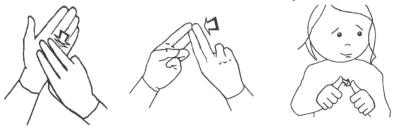

Mummy kiss better.

EXAMPLES OF SIGNS IN EVERYDAY USE

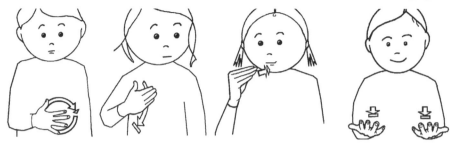

Hungry?..........Want to eat...........now?

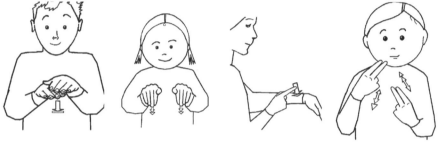

Sit down.......wait.......time for dinner

Enough?.......Like more?

Say please..........good boy/girl

EXAMPLES OF SIGNS IN EVERYDAY USE

Finish   now.................play   later

Upstairs...................bath   time.....

wash hair...towel dry..... nice and warm......

to bed.....   ...kiss kiss.......night night.

AEROPLANE

'Y' hand makes short movement forward/up at head height. Hand may move around in play and 'land' on L. palm for *airport, landing*.

AFTER, AFTERWARDS

Palm down R. closed hand with thumb out, moves in small forward arc over L. flat hand (reverse movement for *before*). **May vary**, see also *next* and *later*.

AFTERNOON

Fingertips of 'N' hand contact chin, then hand twists at the wrist to point forward.

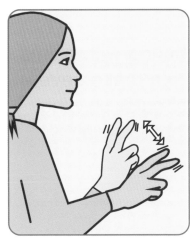

AGAIN, REPEAT

R. 'V' hand with palm facing to the left, makes small repeated shaking movement forward/down.

ALL GONE, FINISHED

Palm up open hands held side by side, move apart in a small arc as the shoulders shrug. There are several signs for *finished* including the sign below.

ALL RIGHT, OK, FINISHED

Closed hands with thumbs up and pointing slightly outwards, move in small outward circles. Can be signed with just one hand. Eyebrows raised for question form.

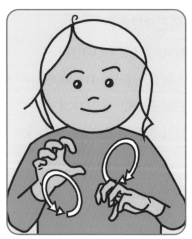

ANIMAL

Clawed hands with palms facing down make several forward circular clawing movements alternately.

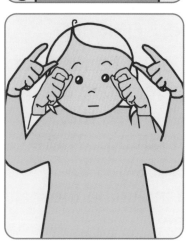

AWAKE, WAKE UP

Index fingers flick upwards off thumbs at sides of eyes.

BABY

One hand rests on top of the other, and hands rock from side to side. Also means *doll*.

BAD

Short forward movement of extended little finger with negative expression. Can be signed with two hands and repeated movement. Sometimes preferred as a sign for *naughty.*

BATH

Open hands (or closed hands) make up and down rubbing movements on the chest **OR** closed hands move in action of using a towel (see page 109).

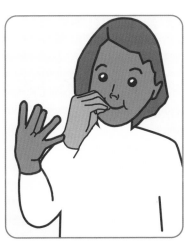

BEAUTIFUL

Full 'O' hand contacts the lips, then hand springs forward as all the fingers open.

BED, SLEEP

The head tilts to rest against the palm of a flat hand. Can be signed with two hands with palms held together. Also used for *cot*.

BEFORE

Flat hand makes small repeated backward movements over the shoulder. Refers to *before*, in the past.

BEHAVE, MANNERS

Flat hands brush alternately down the body in backward circular movements.

BETTER

R. extended thumb brushes forward twice against L. extended thumb.

BIRD: DUCK

Index opens and closes onto thumb several times in front of the mouth in action of a beak. Full hand is used for *duck*.

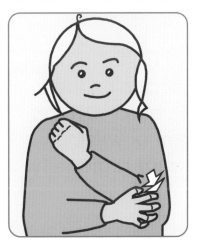

BISCUIT

Fingertips of clawed R. hand tap against the left elbow twice.

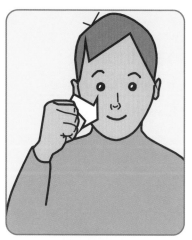

BLACK

Knuckles of closed hand brush forward/down sharply across the cheek. Can be followed by the sign **drink** for **blackcurrant juice.**

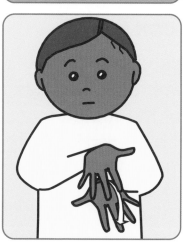

BLOOD

R. open hand moves forward/down across the back of the L. palm down open hand. May start with the index finger touching the lips (see **red**).

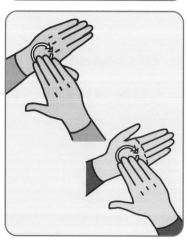

BLUE

Fingers of R. flat hand rub in small circles on the back of L. hand **OR** on the L. palm or wrist. Colours **vary regionally.**

BOIL, BOILING

Extended index fingers make small repeated upward circling movements alternately, like bubbles rising. The cheeks are puffed.

BOOK

Flat hands held together with palms touching twist to open like a book.

BOTTLE, DRINK

Closed hand with thumb extended contacts thumb to mouth. May tilt upwards. Refers to a baby's bottle.

BOY

Extended R. index finger brushes left across chin in single or repeated movement **OR** index and thumb close in small stroking movements on chin.

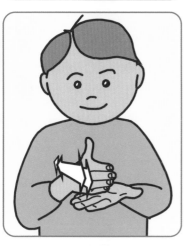

BREAD

Edge of R. flat hand slices to and fro on L. palm   May vary eg *chapati* - palms of open hands tap together, R. onto L. then reverse and repeat.

BREAK, REST

Thumbs of open hands contact upper chest. Head may be tilted to one side. The fingers may wiggle. Means '*take a break, have a rest, relax*'.

BREAK, BROKEN

Fists held together twist apart in snapping action.

BROTHER

Closed hands rub up and down against each other.

BROWN

Fingers of R. hand make small circular rubbing movements on left forearm **OR** clawed hand moves up underside of left forearm. Colours **vary regionally**.

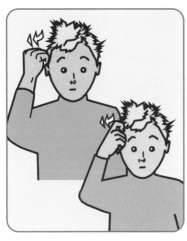

BRUSH (hairbrush): COMB

Closed hand moves in action of using a hair *brush*; Irish 'T' hand for *comb*. Movement is repeated several times for *brush* or *comb your hair.*

BUS

Palm up closed hands make large backwards and forwards steering movements.   Also refers to other large vehicles eg *lorry, van*, and one version of *tractor*.

BUS

Bent 'V' hand makes short forward (or downward) movement near shoulder. Also refers to *tube, underground train*. **Regional.**

CAKE

Fingertips of R. clawed hand tap back of L. flat hand twice.

CAN

Palm back 'C' hand near nose moves forward/down as index finger flexes or closes onto thumb.

CAN'T

Index finger near nose moves down and twists over in crossing out movement as the head shakes.

CAR, DRIVE

Palm back closed hands make small steering movements. **Drive** may also be signed by both hands making short firm forward movement.

CAREFUL, CAREFULLY

Index fingers flex as they move forward/down from near the eyes.

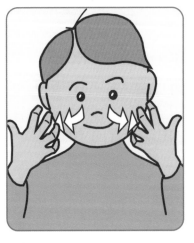

CAT

Fingers flex as hands move out from sides of mouth in repeated movement, to indicate cat's whiskers.

CEREAL, EAT (with a spoon)

Irish 'T' hand makes scooping movements up to the mouth. Represents eating with a spoon, eg *porridge, pudding, soup*, etc. Also means *breakfast.*

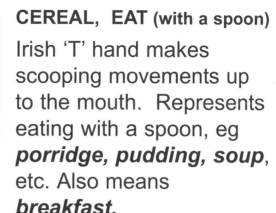

CHANGE

Extended index fingers **OR** Irish 'T' hands twist round from the wrists to change places with each other, palms facing throughout. Handshapes can **vary.**

CLEAN

R. flat hand brushes forward along L. palm **OR** edge of R. flat hand brushes forward twice along L. palm.

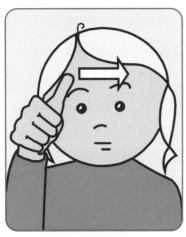

CLEVER

Tip of extended R. thumb moves sharply across the forehead, right to left.

CLOTHES

Open hands brush down the body with short repeated movement. Also means *get dressed*.

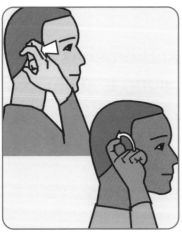

COCHLEAR IMPLANT: HEARING AID

Tips of bent 'V' hand contact side of the head behind the ear for *implant*. Same location, bent index finger twists over ear for *hearing aid.*

COLD (have a cold or 'flu)

Fingers close onto the thumb in wiping action near the nose. Also used for *hanky*.

COLD (feel cold)

Closed hands held in front of body, as elbows pull into body in shivering action.

COLOUR

Palm forward open hand makes small vertical anti-clockwise circles **OR** the same movement with a 'C' hand.

COME, COME HERE

Palm back extended index finger (the index finger may be bent) moves back to self, or may make repeated waggling movement (*come here*).

COOK, COOKER

Irish 'T' hand with palm facing up/in makes repeated short forward movements. Both hands can be used.

COUGH

Index finger edge of fist taps the chest twice. Mouth may be slightly open in action of coughing.

COW

Thumb tips of 'Y' hands at sides of head; hands may remain static or twist from palm down to palm forward. Can be signed with just one hand.

CREAM (eg medicated)

R. flat hand makes small circular rubbing movements on back of left arm, or on the appropriate part of the body.

CRY

Index fingers brush alternately down the cheeks several times. Fingers may flex as they move down.

CUDDLE

Closed hands crossed at the wrists hug into the body as the shoulders are raised and upper body twists slightly from side to side.

CUPBOARD, FRIDGE

Fists move backwards and apart in action of opening a cupboard. Can be signed with one hand only, also meaning *fridge.*

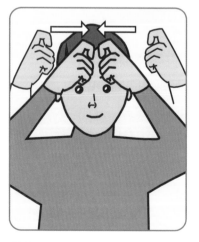

CURTAIN/S

Irish 'T' hands move in action of opening or closing curtains.

CUT (oneself)

The side of R. index finger is drawn across the left forearm, or on the appropriate part of the body.

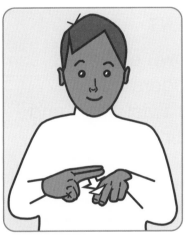

DAD, DADDY, FATHER

Repeated fingerspelt letter 'F' **OR** repeated fingerspelt letter 'D' for *dad* or *daddy* is sometimes used.

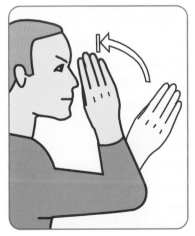

DANGER, DANGEROUS

Index finger edge of R. flat hand comes sharply up to contact forehead. Contact may be repeated.

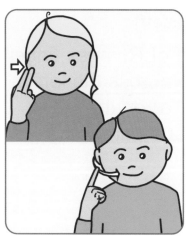

DEAF: HEARING

Deaf is signed with fingertips of 'N' hand contacting the ear.

Hearing is signed with the tip of extended index finger moving from ear to tap on chin.

DIFFERENT

Palm down extended index fingers held together twist apart and over to finish palm up.

DINNER, MEAL

Palm back 'N' hands move alternately up to mouth several times.

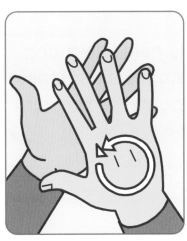

DIRTY

R. open hand rubs in small anti-clockwise circles on L. palm. The nose may be wrinkled.

DIRTY

(Alternative sign) Closed hands crossed at the wrists rub against each other in small circles. The nose may be wrinkled.

DOCTOR

Middle fingertip (or index) and thumb of R. hand tap the L. wrist twice **OR** R. 'O' hand contacts right, then left side of upper chest.

DOG

'N' hands held like a dog in begging position, make small repeated downward movements **OR** flat hand pats the thigh twice (**regional**).

DON'T KNOW

Tips of flat hand touch forehead, then hand swings forward/down to finish palm up as **shoulders shrug and head shakes.**

DON'T LIKE

Open hand on chest moves forward twisting to palm up as **the head shakes. The nose is wrinkled.**

DON'T TOUCH

The head shakes as palm forward open hands start crossed and move emphatically apart, then R. hand makes short movement forward.

DRINK, JUICE, WATER

Full 'C' hand moves to mouth and makes small tipping movement. The sign for *orange* can be added, or appropriate initial letter or colour.

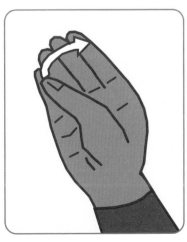

DRY

The thumb starts in contact with little finger and rubs across the pads of the fingertips. Both hands may be used, moving apart.

EASY: HARD

Tip of index finger prods into cheek twice for *easy, simple.* Tip of thumb prods into L. palm twice for *difficult*, *hard.* **Cheeks puffed for emphasis.**

EAT, FOOD

Bunched hand makes small repeated movement towards the mouth. Also means *breakfast, lunch, supper,* etc, distinguished by lip-pattern.

ENOUGH, PLENTY

Back of bent hand brushes forward/up twice underneath the chin.

FALL, FALL OVER

R. 'V' hand stands on L. palm, then R. hand twists and flops down to finish palm up on L. palm.

FAMILY

Palm down open hand moves round in small horizontal circle **OR** the same movement with the fingerspelt 'F' formation as illustrated below.

FAMILY

Fingerspelt 'F' formation moves round in small horizontal circle **OR** palm down open hand makes the same movement as illustrated above.

FAST, EARLY

Extended R. index finger bounces sharply up off L. index once.

FINGERSPELL, SPELL

Finger and thumb tips of bunched hands wiggle against each other as the hands move to the right.

FINISH

Hands move slightly down as fingers snap down onto thumbs. One of several variations. See also *all right* page 43.

FIRE

Fingers wiggle as hands move up and down alternately, palms facing each other **OR** with palms facing back.

FRIEND

R. hand loosely grasps L. and hands shake up and down several times **OR** closed hands with thumbs up bang together twice, also meaning *partner*.

GIRL

Palm forward extended index finger makes small forward brushing movements across the cheek.

GIVE

Palm up flat hand moves forward. Both hands can be used, and handshape and directions may change to suit the **context**. See '**Directional Verbs**' page 26.

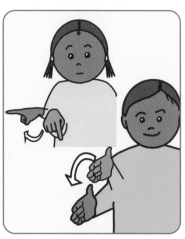

GO

Index finger swings to point forward **OR** a flat hand can be used in same movement, or with palm left, moving forward as shown.

GOOD

Closed hand with thumb up moves slightly forward. Both hands can be used for extra emphasis. Also used as greetings sign *hello.*

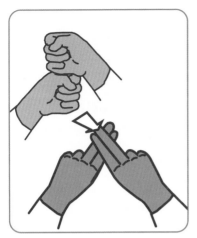

GRANDFATHER, GRANDAD

Hands form fingerspelt 'G' then 'F' **OR** 'G' then 'D' for *grandad*, or other family name sign.

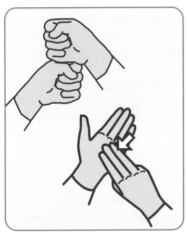

GRANDMOTHER, GRANDMA

Hands form fingerspelt 'G' then 'M'. *Nana* can be spelt out in full, or repeated initial 'N', or other family name sign.

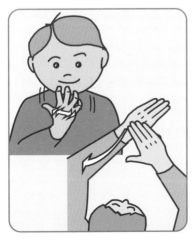

GREEN

Palm back clawed hand shakes side to side near chin **OR** R. flat hand sweeps up left forearm (also means *field*). There are a number of **regional variations** for colours.

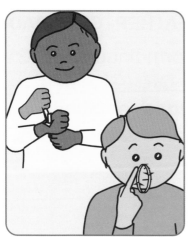

GREEN

Hands make repeated fingerspelt 'G' **OR** index finger makes small circular movements near nose (**regional**).

HAPPY, ENJOY

Flat hands brush against each other twice with smiling expression.

HAVE, HAD, GOT

Slightly clawed hand, palm up, makes small movement down as it snaps shut closing sharply to a fist.

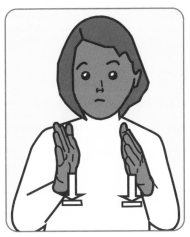

HAVE TO, MUST

Palm facing flat hands move down firmly with emphasis.

HELLO, HI

Palm forward hand moves to the right in a small arc. There are several variations, see also *good* page 70.

HELP

R. closed hand rests on L. palm and hands move forward in '*I'll help you*' or back in '*help me*' etc depending on context. See '**Directional Verbs**' page 26.

HOME

Fingertips of flat hands contact each other at an angle. May move apart and down in outline shape, also meaning *house*.

HORSE

Closed hands, one on top of the other **OR** side by side, make short repeated movements forward/down.

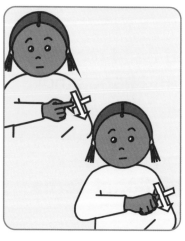

HOSPITAL

R. index finger tip **OR** thumb tip, draws a cross on the left upper arm.

There are a number of other variations used in the adult community.

HOT

Palm back clawed hand is drawn sharply left to right in front of the mouth. Also means *heat, heating*. Fingerspelt initial 'C' followed by this sign for *central heating*.

HOUSE

Fingers of 'N' hands contact at an angle, then move apart/down in outline shape of building. Flat hands can also be used.

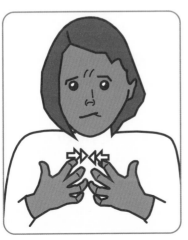

HOW

Fingers held open and bent, tap knuckles twice. Can be held palm up or palm back as shown.

HUNGRY

Open hand rubs in circles **OR** closed hand rubs up and down on the stomach. There are several other versions of this sign.

HURT, PAIN, PAINFUL, SORE

Palm back open hands shake alternately up and down. Relevant part of the body can be indicated by pointing, eg the ear, the throat, the knee etc.

ICE-CREAM

Closed hand makes two small downward movements near the mouth, as the tongue slightly protrudes.

ILL, UNWELL

Edges of little fingers brush down the chest, cheeks puffed for emphasis.

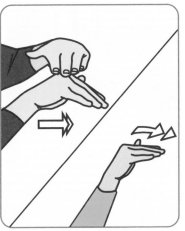

INSIDE: OUTSIDE

R. bent hand makes two short forward movements under L. hand for *inside*. R. bent hand makes two short forward movements at shoulder height for *outside*.

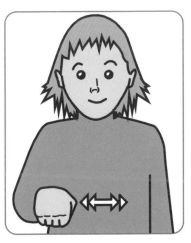

IRON

Closed hand moves in action of holding and moving an iron from side to side.

JUMP, BABY BOUNCER

Fingers of R. 'V' hand flex and straighten as they bounce up and down on L. palm.

KETTLE

'Y' hand moves inward in small arc, or makes small tipping movement. Can vary for different types of kettle.

KEY

Irish 'T' hand twists at the wrist in action of holding and using a key. May twist firmly clockwise for *lock* and anti-clockwise for *unlock*.

KISS, BLOW A KISS

Tips of R. 'N' hand contact tips of L. Hands may twist and reverse positions and repeat. Flat hand touches puckered lips then twists forward/down for **blow a kiss.**

KISS

Tips of R. bunched hand touch the mouth, then contact the tips of L. bunched hand.

KNOW

Tip of extended thumb taps side of forehead twice.

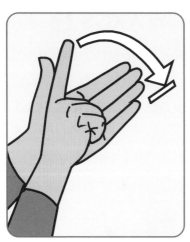

LATE

Extended R. index finger pivots sharply forward/down against L. palm.

LATER, AFTER

Index finger pointing up with palm forward, twists to the right in a small arc. Can be two small movements. Also means *afterwards*.

LEAVE, GO

Flat hand swings forward/right from palm back to palm down.

LIE DOWN

R. 'V' hand rests palm up on L. palm and makes a short movement to the right.

LIGHT, LIGHT ON

Full 'O' hand springs open and down near the head. Repeat for flashing light. Can change direction and location to suit context.

LIGHT OFF

Fingers open and pointing downwards snap shut in small upward movement near the head, or in location and direction to suit the context.

LOVELY, NICE

Back of extended thumb is drawn across the chin from left to right.

MANY, LOTS

Palm back hands move apart with fingers wiggling, cheeks puffed for emphasis. With questioning raised eyebrows, means *how many?*

MAYBE, PERHAPS

'Y' hand makes quick repeated waggling movements from the wrist.

MEDICINE

R. Irish 'T' hand moves upwards to mouth from L. full 'C' hand.

MILK

Palm back 'Y' hands make alternate short up and down movements. See also variations below.

MILK

Hand makes short up and down movements with squeezing action, both hands may be used with alternate movements **OR** closed hands with thumbs up rub together.

MORE

R. flat hand moves back to tap twice against the back of L. flat hand. Both hands are palm back.

MORNING

Tips of R. bent hand contact left then right upper chest **OR** tips of two bent hands contact the waist, then brush upwards on the body.

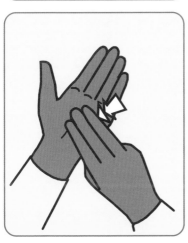

MOTHER, MUM, MUMMY

R. 'M' hand taps twice on L. palm. See also the following variation.

MOTHER, MUM, MUMMY

Fingers of R. 'M' hand (or flat hand) tap the side of the forehead twice (**regional**). See also the previous illustration.

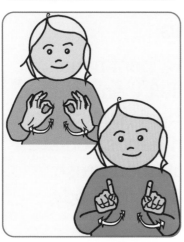

MUSIC

Palm forward 'O' hands swing in and out towards each other several times **OR** the same movement with extended index fingers.

NAME, CALLED

Fingers of 'N' hand touch side of forehead, then move and twist forward/down.

NAPPY

Fingers snap closed onto thumbs against sides of body. 'N' hands can be used, or other variation relevant to type of nappy in context.

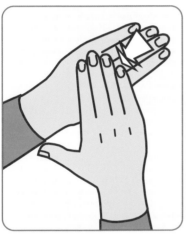

NAUGHTY

R. flat hand taps back of L. twice **OR** the little finger extended from closed hand makes two short forward movements (see **bad** page 45).

NEXT, AFTER, TURN

Closed hand with thumb out twists over from palm down to palm up in sideways or forward movement, to suit context.

NIGHT, DARK

Palm back flat hands swing in/down to cross each other.   Reverse movement for *day, light*.

NO

Closed (or flat) hand twists sharply from the wrist as the head shakes (can be just the headshake alone). The arm can be outstretched within child's line of vision.

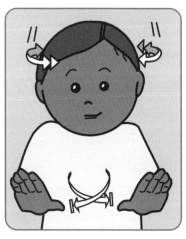

NO, NOT, DON'T

Hands start crossed with palms facing forward/down; hands uncross and swing sharply apart as the head shakes with emphasis. Also means *not allowed.*

NOISE, NOISY

Index finger makes forward circular movements near the ear.

NOT YET

Palm forward closed hands make small shaking movements towards each other as the head shakes.

NOW, TODAY

Palm up open hands make short sharp movement down, also meaning *at once, right now.* Repeated movement for *today*.

LIKE

Flat hand taps chest twice (also means *front*). Open hand on chest moves forward closing with index up to mean *if you like, please yourself.*

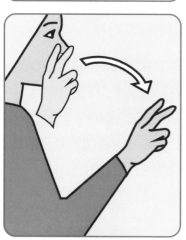

LOOK, WATCH

'V' hand moves forward from near eye, or can be located and/or moved in direction to suit context (fingers represent direction of eye-gaze). See page 27.

LOVE

Hands held crossed move back to contact the chest.

NURSERY

Tip of extended middle finger makes two small downward brushing movements on the chin. There are other variations including the first sign for *school* on page 99.

ORANGE (colour and fruit)

Clawed hand makes small squeezing movements near side of mouth. Can be followed by the sign for *drink* for *orange juice*.

PARK, SWINGS

Closed hands make several forward and back swinging movements simultaneously.

PARK

Index finger edge of flat hand taps twice against the upper chest. This is also a **regional** sign for *green*, and for *school*.

PARTY, HAVE FUN

'O' hands move up and down alternately to the mouth **OR** 'Y' hands at shoulder height move in and out in circular movements, twisting from the wrists.

PIG

Index finger edge of fist brushes nose, as hand moves in small repeated circular movements.

PLASTER

The pad of extended R. thumb moves across the back of L. hand, or the appropriate part of the body in context.

PLAY

Palm up open hands move in repeated upward circular movements simultaneously.

PLEASE, THANK YOU

Fingertips of flat hand touch chin, then hand drops forward/down to finish palm up. Sometimes both hands are used for extra emphasis for *many thanks, grateful* etc.

PLUG, SOCKET

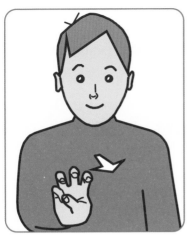

Index, middle and ring fingers extended and bent; hand makes short movement forward.

POO

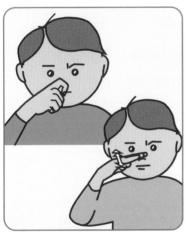

Grasp the nose with index finger and thumb, or make small up and down waving movements in front of the nose. Also means *smell, smelly*. Alternatively, fingerspell 'POO'.

POORLY, SICK

Flat hand brushes across the forehead. The head may tilt to one side.

POTTY

R. index finger pointing down makes horizontal circle slightly above and to the right of L. fist.

PUSHCHAIR, BUGGY

Two fists make forward pushing movement.

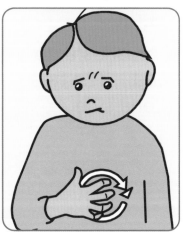

QUEASY, FEEL SICK

Clawed hand moves in circles on the stomach, or lower chest. Used for feeling *unease, upset tummy* etc. The tongue may protrude slightly.

QUICK, BE QUICK, HURRY

Extended R. index finger bounces sharply up off L. in quick repeated movements. Means *hurry up, quickly* and so on.

QUIET (be quiet), HUSH, SH

Index finger is held to the lips, then two palm forward 'O' hands move slowly apart.

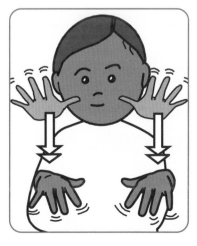

RAIN

Palm down open hands move down in repeated movement in front of the body. Can be modified to show fast or heavy rain and the cheeks may be puffed for emphasis.

READ

R. 'V' hand moves from side to side across the L. palm or with direction and movement to suit the context **OR** flat hands held like a book move slightly from side to side.

READY, GET READY

Thumbs of open hands tap twice (**OR** make short upward brushing movements) against sides of upper chest. Also means *already*.

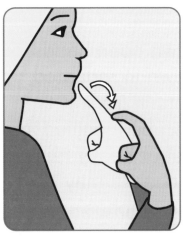

RED

Extended index finger makes short movement forward/down from the mouth as it bends. May repeat.

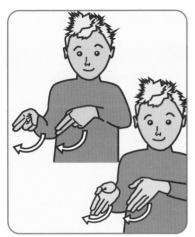

ROAD, STREET

Palm facing 'N' hands swivel from the wrists from pointing down to pointing forward **OR** the same movement with flat hands.

RUN

Fists swing forward and back alternately at sides of body in action of arms when running.

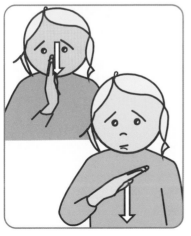

SAD

Index edge of palm left flat hand brushes down the nose **OR** the index edge of palm down flat hand brushes down the chest. The shoulders and mouth droop.

SAFE, SAFELY

Edge of R. bent hand rests on L. palm as both hands move back to body. Also means **protect**.

SAME, LIKE

Extended index fingers pointing forward tap together. Also means **also, too**.

SAND

Thumbs rub across the pads of the fingers as the hands move slightly upwards.

SAY, TELL

Index finger moves forward from the mouth.

SCHOOL

Palm back flat hand **OR** palm forward 'N' hand makes short side to side movements in front of mouth.

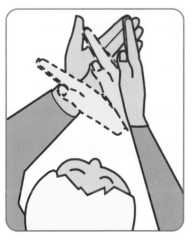

SHARE, SHARE OUT

Edge of R. flat hand chops down several times across the L. palm twisting slightly round/forward. Meaning to share something eg cake, several ways.

SHARE

Edge of R. flat hand rocks slightly on L. palm as hands move forward and back. Means to share eg a toy or food between two. R. hand slices across L. palm for *half, part*.

SHEEP

Extended little fingers make forward circling movements near sides of head. One hand can be used.

SHOP, SHOPPING

Bent hands make two short movements down. **Regional** sign.

Irish 'T' hand brushes down L. palm twice for *shopping, buying.*

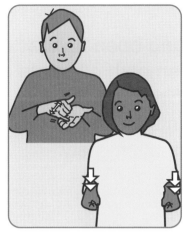

SHOP, SHOPPING

R. 'Y' hand makes small side to side rubbing movements on L. palm. **Regional** sign.

Fists make repeated small up and down movements near hips for **shopping.**

SHY

Tip of R. index on chin twists from palm left to palm back. Head is slightly tilted.

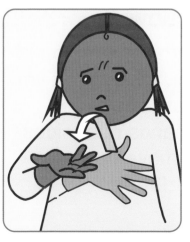

SICK, VOMIT

Open hand brushes up the body and forward from the mouth as it twists to palm up.

SIGN

Palm facing open hands move in smooth alternate forward circling movements **OR** move up and down alternately.

SISTER

Bent index finger taps twice against the nose.

SIT, SIT DOWN

Flat hands, one on top of the other, make short firm movement down **OR** closed hands near sides of body move down, or other **variation**.

SLEEP

Index fingers close onto thumbs as hands move in slightly at the sides of the eyes. Can be all the fingers closing into bunched hands.

SLOW, SLOWLY

R. flat hand moves slowly up left forearm. Extended index finger may also be used, also meaning *long time*. Palm down open hand waves downwards twice for *slow down*.

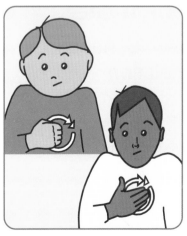

SORRY, APOLOGISE

Closed hand **OR** flat hand rubs in circles on chest. There are several other **variations**.

SORRY, OOPS

Clawed hand shakes backwards and forwards several times at the side of the head **OR** near the chin. The shoulders lift. Also means *accident, mistake*.

START, BEGIN

R. closed hand with thumb extended brushes sharply down behind palm back L. flat hand.

STAY, STOP THERE

Palm down 'C' hands make small firm movement down, or towards the person or pet for example. One hand can be used.

STOP

Fingers snap shut onto thumb. Both hands may be used. One of several **variations**.

STOP, HANG ON, WAIT

Hand makes short firm movement forward - movement may be repeated. Both hands can be used.

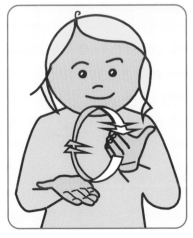

STORY

Flat hands rotate round each other in forward circular movements.   Also means *explain, tell about.*

SUN, SUNNY

Full 'O' hand at head height moves slightly down/left and opens. Can change direction in context.

SWIM

Flat hands move in forward circular movements in the action of swimming (breast stroke) **OR** arms can move in overarm strokes.

TEACHER

Index fingers make two short repeated forward movements forward/apart from the sides of the mouth.

TELEVISION, SCREEN

Extended index fingers move in outline shape of a television screen. Alternatively fingerspell 'TV'.

THIRSTY, DRY

Fingers and thumb on throat move forward as fingers close onto the thumb to form a bunched hand.

TIDY, TIDY UP

Palm facing flat hands make short downward movement, then move to the right and repeat.

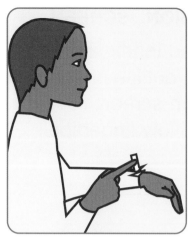

TIME, WHAT TIME?

R. index finger taps the back of L. wrist twice. The eyebrows are raised to give question form *what time?*

TIRED

Thumbtips of open hands rest on upper chest as hands flop down and twist over to finish palm up. Cheeks may be puffed for emphasis and head tilted.

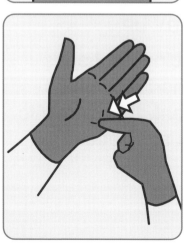

TOILET

Repeat fingerspelt initial 'T'.

TOMORROW: YESTERDAY

Index finger on side of cheek swings forward/down to finish palm up for *tomorrow, next day*. The finger drops down/back to touch shoulder for *yesterday.*

TOWEL, BATH

Closed hands move in action of holding and using a bath towel, and refers to *towel,* an alternative sign for *bath*, and also *dry with a bathtowel*.

TOY

Hands in fingerpelt initial 'T' formation move inwards in small circular movements **OR** fingerspell 'TOY'

TRAIN

Closed hand moves in small forward circles at side of body **OR** makes short firm forward movement.

TREE

R. open hand makes repeated twisting movements from the wrist, with elbow resting on L. hand.

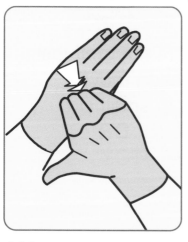

TROUBLE, BOTHER

Fingertips of R. bent hand tap back of L. hand **OR** forearm, twice.

UP: DOWN

Index finger points and makes short movement up for *up,* and points and moves down for *down.* Movements are repeated for *upstairs* and *downstairs*.

WAIT

Bent hands make two short movements down **OR** closed hands make repeated inward circles.

WALK

R. index and middle fingers move in action of legs walking across the L. palm **OR** bent 'V' hand brushes forward twice along L. palm.

WANT, NEED

Flat hand on side of upper chest makes small firm movement down, twisting to palm down.

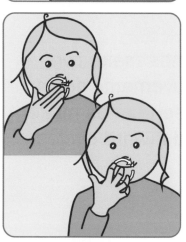

WARM

Palm back flat hand **OR** clawed hand makes small circular movements in front of the mouth.

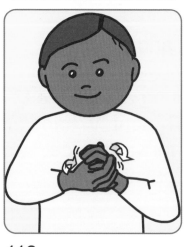

WASH, SOAP

Hands rub together in washing action (*wash hands*). Open hand moves round the face in circular motion for *face wash*, or on the appropriate part of the body.

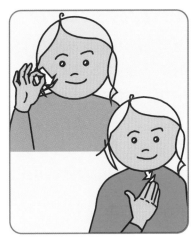

WATER, THIRSTY

Tips of 'O' hand brush forward/down cheek twice **OR** fingertips of R. bent hand brush down throat twice (**regional,** also meaning *thirsty*).

WATER, SEA

Palm down open hand makes small wavy up and down movements as it moves to the right.

WEE WEE

Repeat fingerspelt initial 'W'. Alternatively, fingerspell 'WEE'

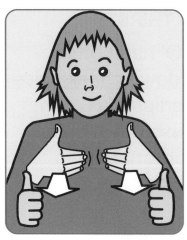

WELL, HOW ARE YOU?

Tips of bent hands touch chest, then hands move forward and close with thumbs up. Also used as greetings sign *how are you? are you well?* with **raised eyebrows**.

WET, DAMP

Fingers of R. hand close onto thumb several times. Both hands can be used.

WHAT?

Palm forward extended index finger shakes in short quick side to side movements. **Eyebrows raised or furrowed for question form.**

WHEN?

Fingers wiggle against side of chin. **Eyebrows raised or furrowed for question form.**

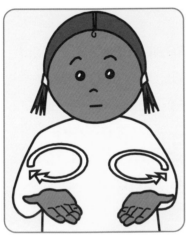

WHERE?

Palm up open hands move in small flat outward circular movements. **Eyebrows raised or furrowed for question form.**

WHICH?

'Y' hand makes small side-to-side movements (directional). **Eyebrows raised or furrowed for question form.**

WHITE
Tip of index finger **OR** 'O' hand make small downward brushing movements on the side of the upper chest, or other **regional variation**.

WHO?
Index finger makes small horizontal circles, palm back **OR** taps chin twice, palm left. **Eyebrows raised or furrowed for question form.**

WHY?
Edge of R. index finger taps left side of chest twice. Also means *because, reason*. **Eyebrows raised or furrowed for question form.**

WIRE

'O' hands start in contact then pull apart, twisting a little from the wrists.   Also means *string.* Can also be signed with the 'O' hands just moving apart.

WORK

R. flat hand chops down twice onto L. at right angles.   Also means *job*.

YELLOW

Open hand makes several short repeated twisting movements at side of head **OR** repeat fingerspelt initial 'Y'. Colours **vary regionally**.

YES

The closed hand nods up and down echoing the nodding of the head. Can be signed with just the **head nod** alone for affirmation.

YOU: ME

Point to person concerned with small forward movement for *you, he she* etc. or with sideways sweep for several people eg *they, them*. Point to self for *me*.

YOUR: MY

Palm forward closed hand moves towards person concerned for *your, yours, her, his,* etc. or sweeps sideways for plural eg *theirs*. Contacts signer's chest for *mine, my*.

SIGNING WITH BABIES

In America extensive research has been carried out on the benefits of using some simple signs (derived from genuine sign language, such as BSL) with hearing babies, in order to communicate with them before they are able to express themselves verbally.

Recent research suggests that babies are learning about the foundations of language and making important connections long before it was previously believed, they just don't have the tools or skills necessary for communicating them. This often results in temper tantrums due to the sheer frustration at not being able to make their needs known or being misunderstood. Using signs can help eliminate this frustration as your baby's needs are more easily communicated and understood and therefore, met by the caregiver.

And because a baby is able to make simple hand gestures and movements before being able to master the complex skills of speech and language, Baby Signs make perfect sense.

As a parent, I have experienced the wonderful benefits of Baby Signing for myself. My daughters were able to tell me if they were hungry, thirsty, hurt, if they needed my help, if they had heard a car or a plane, or seen a bird or a cat, all before they could say the words. I will always look back upon my daughters' signing days with great fondness and enthusiasm. I have gained much insight into a baby's world with a deep sense of understanding and knowledge that there really is a lot more to babies then I ever realised before. I will forever be grateful for being able to share in my both my daughters' thoughts and feelings at such a tender age.

As a teacher of the Baby Signing concept I am actively encouraging the use of BSL signs, rather than made up signs (or ASL signs). I strongly believe that using the 'language of the Deaf' is the way forward and makes much more sense. Not only will these babies be able to communicate with their parents and caregivers, they will also have the basics of signing that they can use with others whose main form of communication is through sign language. Most importantly, they will gain an extremely valuable awareness and understanding of the form of communication used by many Deaf and/or special needs persons. This, I hope, will help a little to bridge the gap between the Deaf and hearing communities.

I will certainly endeavour to encourage both of my own daughters to continue to sign, even though they are at the ages where speech is their most prominent form of communication. One day, should the need arise, they will be able to communicate (on a very basic level) with a signing deaf child or adult, and that will really warm my heart. I shall certainly feel that signing with them has been even more worthwhile than I ever thought it would be. I am very grateful for being able to share in this wonderful language and will continue to encourage my students to realise the importance and value of sign language and to consider learning a little more about it as I have done. Maybe someday my students might meet a signer and be able to experience the thrill of conversing with them and hopefully sharing just a little piece of their world.

Adèle Marshall

www.happysigners.co.uk

To find out more about babysigning, materials, and trade terms for classes, contact DeafBooks.co.uk (full details page 123).

SUGGESTED FURTHER READING AND RESOURCES

The LET'S SIGN: BSL Series of Resources:
DeafBooks.co.uk (See details and images page 131)

Let's Sign Dictionary: 2nd Edition Revised & Enlarged.
C. Smith (2009). Co-Sign Communications: Stockton-on-Tees.

Deaf Children at Home. J. Kyle and H. Sutherland (1993).
Centre for Deaf Studies, University of Bristol.

The Care and Education of a Deaf Child: *A Book for Parents*. (Parents' and Teachers' Guides). Pamela Knight,
Ruth Swanwick. (1999). Multilingual Matters.

Issues in Deaf Education. Susan Gregory (Editor), Stephen
Powers (Editor), Linda Watson (Editor), Pamela Knight
(Editor), Wendy McCracken (Editor) (1998). David Fulton
Publishers.

Sign Bilingualism: A Model. M. Pickersgill, S. Gregory
(1998).

The **National Deaf Children's Society (NDCS)** provide a
range of helpful publications for parents and professionals on
communication, education, audiology, technology and welfare
benefits including:

**Supporting the achievement of deaf children in the early
years.**

**Supporting the achievement of deaf children in primary
schools.**

**Supporting the achievement of deaf young people in
further education.**

Most publications are free of charge to parents of deaf children
and most are available to download from www.ndcs.org.uk

122

Useful Contacts

British Association of Teachers of the Deaf (BATOD)
National Executive Officer and Magazine Editor:
Paul Simpson
Tel: 0845 6435181
e-mail: exec@batod.org.uk
web: www.batod.org.uk

British Deaf Association (BDA)
18 Leather Lane, London, EC1N 7SU
Tel/Voice: 0207 405 0090
e-mail: bda@bda.org.uk
web: www.bda.org.uk

BSL for Kids
Mobile Application Development and Sign/Symbol
Materials for Special Needs and Mainstream
Tel: +44 (0) 1274 875257
Fax: +44 (0) 7771 571109
e-mail: michelle@BSLforKids.co.uk
web: www.BSLforKids.co.uk

Co-Sign Communications
(inc. DeafBooks & Deafsign)
For the Let's Sign Series
16 Highfield Crescent, Hartburn,
Stockton-on-Tees TS18 5HH.
Tel: 01642 580505
e-mail: cath@deafsign.com
web: www.deafsign.com
web: www.DeafBooks.co.uk

The National Deaf Children's Society   (NDCS)
National Office, 15 Dufferin Street,
London EC1Y 8UR.
Freephone Helpline:
Mon-Fri 10am - 5pm 0808 800 8880
Fax: 020 7251 5020
Switchboard Tel: 020 7490 8656
e-mail: helpline@ndcs.org.uk
web: www.ndcs.org.uk

Signature
Mersey House, Mandale Business Park,
Belmont, Durham DH1 3UZ.
Tel: 0191 383 1155
Text: 0191 383 7915   **Fax:** 0191 383 7914
e-mail: durham@signature.org.uk
web: www.signature.org.uk

USEFUL WEBSITES

www.itvbabysign.com   www.mybslbooks.com

www.deafparent.org.uk   www.deafsign.com

www.signedstories.com   www.DeafBooks.co.uk

www.signstation.org   www.BSLforKids.co.uk

www.familysignlanguage.org.uk

www.ucl.ac.uk/HCS/research/EBSLD

INDEX

126

127

LET'S SIGN

SERIES of British Sign Language (BSL) resources and materials for all ages and abilities.
Compatible with all educational sign systems based on BSL.

EARLY YEARS & BABY SIGNS:
A3 POSTERS 1&2

48 of the most useful First Signs
Signs include **'bath' 'bed' 'milk'**
'more' 'hurt' 'cuddle'.

Also available on
FLASHCARDS

LET'S SIGN FAMILY TOPICS
A4 format, slide-bound 60 page 383 illustrations

The 36 topics include My Family, Out and About, My House, At the Nursery, Food and Drink, Bed Time, Useful Phrases and many more.

LET'S SIGN & DOWN SYNDROME
A4 format, slide-bound 58 page 280 illustrations
arranged in topics including Family, Feelings, Health, Actions/Instructions, Home, School, Manners and Time.

Bold and eye-catching laminated
A2 Poster - BSL Greeting Signs
BSL and Deaf Awareness raising in Nurseries, Schools,
Colleges, Hospitals and all Public Buildings.
Suitable for anywhere and everywhere.

Colourful wipe-clean and in topics
A4 POSTER/MATS (4)
'Greetings' ' Family' ' Feelings' ' Questions'
Other topics can be added on request
Also available in
Bengali, Gujarati, Urdu and German

◆

HOUSE & HOME FLASHCARDS

50 cards (4" x 6")
Large image of sign and word on one side.
Fingerspelt word and description on reverse.

◆

BSL REWARD STICKERS

Signs to reward and motivate. 'Well done' 'Brilliant'
'Good work' 'Gold star' etc.

**See also our latest BSL iphone
and ipad apps on the Apple
Store or contact us for details.**

LET'S SIGN DICTIONARY
Everyday BSL for Learners
2nd Edition Revised & Enlarged (A4)

The most recommended resource for

- BSL Courses

- Services

- Schools

- Families

300 pages • 2,400 signs • 6,000 word Index.
The largest collection of contemporary BSL signs in print.

LET'S SIGN POCKET
DICTIONARY (A6)

404 pages with over 1,000 illustrated
useful signs with descriptions.

LET'S SIGN Songs for Children
Popular Songs to Sign-a-long to

Book and DVD

17 Songs and rhymes with British
Sign Language (BSL) signs for all
children in mainstream settings to
enjoy together.

INTRODUCTION TO BSL CURRICULUM FOR EARLY YEARS

Tutor Book & Student (A4)

Excellent introduction to BSL for Early Years settings - for complete beginners, schools and families.

Tutor Book with lessons plans, and materials plus CDrom containing extra teaching resources.

Student Book with structured lessons, worksheets and activities.

(Required course material for all students).

LET'S SIGN GRAPHICS

New signs and commissioned work also available.

We work with other writers and developers who use the Let's Sign graphics in their materials.

We also work in collaboration with services such as Health, Education, Housing and Local Councils to develop accessible information using the sign graphics on notices and text to support communication.

See the full Let's Sign Series - plus games and
FREE DOWNLOADS
www.DeafBooks.co.uk
contact: cath@deafsign.com - 01642 580505
